P9-CDB-834

DRAWN THREADWORK

DRAWN THREADWORK

Lisa Melen

Edited by
Lynette de Denne

 VAN NOSTRAND REINHOLD
NEW YORK   CINCINNATI   LONDON   TORONTO   MELBOURNE

This book was originally published
in Swedish under the titles Näversöm
and Modeller i Näversöm by I.C.A.
Förlaget Västerås, Sweden

Näversöm copyright © Lisa Melen and
I.C.A. Forlaget 1968
Modeller i Näversöm © Lisa Melen and
I.C.A. Forlaget 1969

Translated from Swedish by Joan Bulman
English translation © Van Nostrand
Reinhold Company Ltd. 1972

Library of Congress Catalog Card Number
70-156128
ISBN 0 442 05308 8

All photographs by Bertil Lindh
except on pages 6, 8 Nordiska Museet and
9, 11 Hallings Foto.

This book is set in Apollo and is
printed in Great Britain by
Jolly & Barber Ltd., Rugby
and bound by the Ferndale
Book Company

Published by Van Nostrand
Reinhold Company, Inc.
450 West 33rd St. New York
N.Y. 10001
and Van Nostrand Reinhold Company Ltd.
Windsor House, 46 Victoria Street,
London S.W.1

Published simultaneously in
Canada by Van Nostrand Reinhold
Company Ltd.

16   15   14   13   12   11   10   9   8   7   6   5   4   3   2   1

CONTENTS

History   7

Materials   13

Preparatory work   15

Technique   18

    Darning Stitch   18

    Diagonal Stitch   26

    Goose-eye Stitch   30

    Ground Stitch   32

    Samplers   36

Making Up   39

Original Designs   42

Designs   48

Suppliers   96

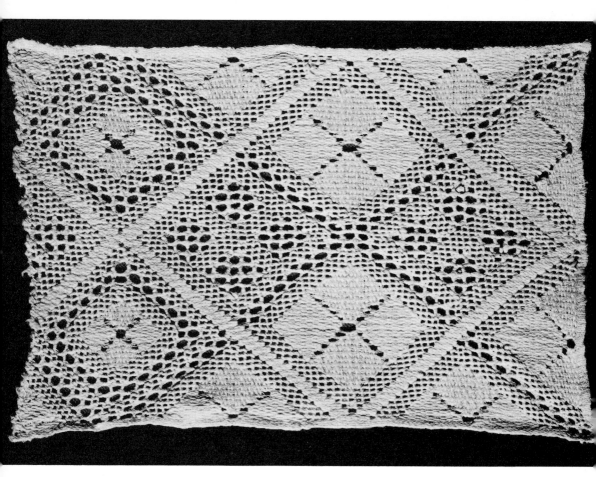

Drawn threadwork represents half the decorative panel of a cushion cover from Hälsingland. Worked in white cotton on a half linen fabric

HISTORY

Drawn threadwork is a method of stitchery worked on a fabric from which threads have been drawn out from both warp and weft. It has been used to decorate linen in the northern provinces of Sweden since the 17th century and there are well preserved articles of clothing and church textiles dating from this period. In the north the stitchery was in pink, red, blue or white, depending on the province, whereas in the south the stitchery was in white thread. An illustration of a cushion cover from the Nordiska Museum in Stockholm, is shown on page 6. The patterns were usually made up of simple geometrical shapes such as rectangles, squares and triangles, or, sometimes, hearts and stars. The Swedish name for drawn threadwork is Näversöm which means, literally, 'birch bark embroidery'. The name derives from the fact that originally a piece of linen was stretched over a strip of birch bark to carry out the work. If the linen used was closely woven, threads were drawn out from both warp and weft to form a lattice work; if loosely woven, the stitching was done direct. It was also not unknown for the ground fabric to be woven over the piece of birch bark by the simple method of looping the warp and weft threads over the edge of the bark. This 'birch bark' embroidery was light and convenient to carry about. When the girls went out to the pastures to mind the cows they took their roll of birch bark in their pockets and the

Above. Cushion cover in drawn thread-work dated 1846. From Jarbo, Finnäs, Gästrikland. The ground work is in white cotton thread on a linen fabric, with the pattern in a thread of pink cotton.

Opposite. Cloth, decorated with drawn threadwork, brought from Russia and now in the Östersund Museum.

craft must have kept them pleasantly occupied through their long solitary days. Here they stitched patterns they had seen in neighbouring farm houses but they also made up their own designs of wreaths, crowns, flowers and leaves. It was characteristic of all Swedish peasant art that even though patterns existed, these were never copied slavishly but with a large measure of freedom for originality.

There are plenty of beautiful interesting examples of drawn threadwork in museums all over Sweden, including one unusual cloth in the Östersund Museum which was brought back from Russia (see page 9). In

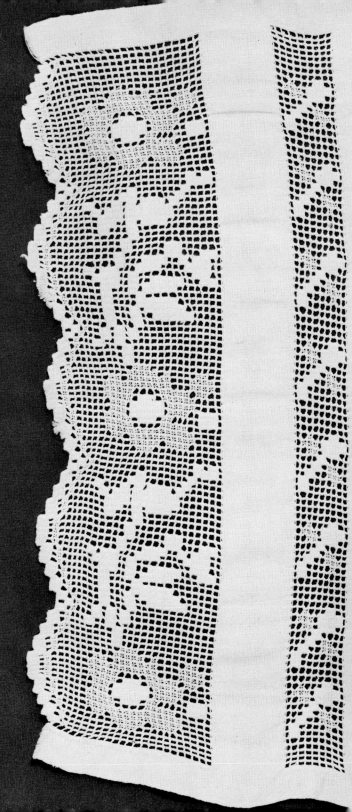

1920, an exhibition in Östersund showed examples of drawn threadwork used as borders on tablecloths, as decoration on lampshades and as wide borders on linen hangings edged with pillow lace. The craft was also used to border sheets and pillow cases and to decorate bridegrooms' shirts. Many churches in northern Sweden have well preserved altar cloths embellished with drawn threadwork. The long bier-bands (by which the coffin was lowered into the earth) made by the peasant women also often had a border of drawn threadwork. These bier-bands were about $3\frac{1}{4}$ yards long and about 15 inches wide and were kept hanging on a special hook in the 'best room', ready to be used on the last journey (see page 11).

At the end of the 18th and the beginning of the 19th century it seems that when the girls from Jämtland and Härjedalen took their spinning-wheels on their backs and made their way down to Hälsingland and Medelpad, they learnt to dress flax and had to weave these samples. In the winter they carded and spun wool and in the summer they tended the cattle in the outlying farms. It was during these days in the 'great forest' that they wove fringes and embroidered borders with their names and the year. To save having to carry the whole length around with them, they used to cut off the ends of the bier-bands and when the work was finished the ends were sewn together again.

Drawn threadwork was first popularised towards the end of the 19th century by a Miss Augusta Gripenberg who owned a needlework shop in Hudiksvall in Sweden. She revived the work before the 'cottage industry' movement began and worked out new designs with such names as 'Crown Robe', 'Evening Star', 'Margit's Rose' and 'Joy'. Her niece inherited an interest in the craft and designed new patterns based on traditional ones. A pupil of Augusta Gripenberg continued with research, lectured extensively and made a list of all

Opposite. A bier-band.

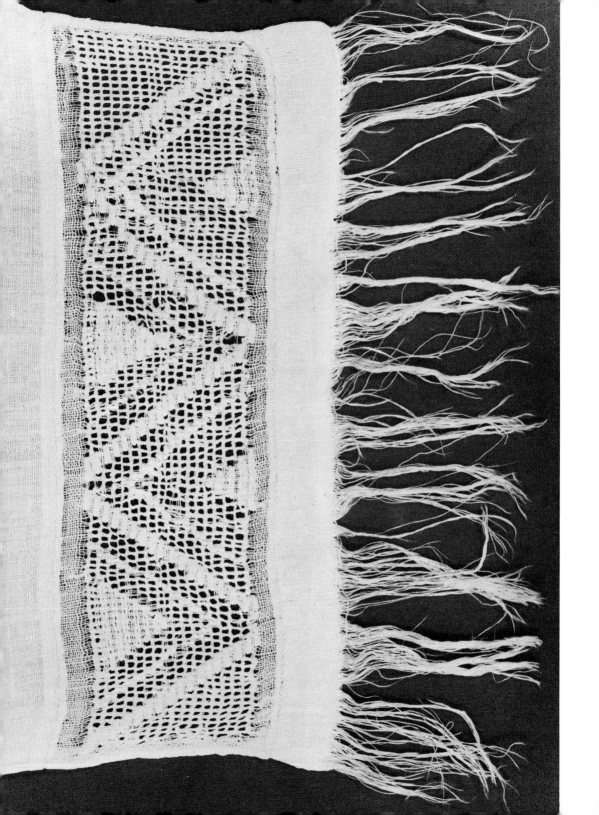

existing specimens of drawn threadwork. The earliest example, dating back to about the beginning of the 18th century, was found wrapped round a roll of birch bark. Recently, drawn threadwork has been included in the syllabuses of adult education organisations in Sweden, special encouragement being given to the creation of original designs.

MATERIALS

1. A piece of soft board for mounting the fabric before
   working the stitchery. It should be 1 inch larger
   than the completed work, about $\frac{1}{2}$ inch thick and
   soft enough to take a needle through at the edges.
   It will be referred to throughout as the pin board.
2. Glass-headed pins, either coloured paper, plastic,
   adhesive paper or a closely-woven fabric.
3. A blunt-pointed tapestry needle size 18 or 20.
4. Evenweave linen. Various linens are suitable for
   drawn threadwork but it is essential that the fabric
   is evenweave, that is, that the number of threads per
   inch is equal in the warp and weft. The weaving
   must be regular and the threads should be strong
   enough to be drawn out easily.
5. Graph paper with 10 squares to the inch.
6. Threads:
   Heavy thread for darning stitch and diagonal
   stitch. Fine thread for ground stitch and goose-eye
   stitch. Very fine sewing thread for hemming.

The threads used for the stitchery depend on the basic
fabric and on the stitch being used: coarse material
requires coarse threads and fine material requires
fine threads. It is also possible to make a pattern stand
out more clearly by using different thicknesses of
thread on the same fabric. It will be necessary to experiment at first to find out suitable threads for different

fabrics. As can be seen from the diagrams, darning stitch and diagonal stitch are usually worked with a double thread in the needle and the stitches need to fill the spaces. Ground stitch and goose-eye are worked with a single thread which should be about the thickness of the thread of the woven material, so that the pattern is created by the holes rather than by the stitches. The technique is very suitable for making up original designs and one should also experiment with different materials.

Most of the examples illustrated are worked on evenweave linen with 34 threads to the inch. Other linens which will be found useful have 19, 23, 25, 26 or 30 threads to the inch. Embroidery threads which may be used for this embroidery include: Linen thread 16/2; Linen lace thread 40, 50 or 60; Coton perlé numbers 5, 8 or 12.

PREPARATORY WORK

If you are working from a pattern the mesh of linen, the size of work and number of holes are always given. If you are making up a pattern, the number of holes per inch in the fabric must be calculated very carefully.

The material must be cut large enough to leave a margin of $1\frac{1}{4}$ inches round the lattice work of holes. It is by this margin that the work is stitched to the pin board. First of all, cut away any selvedges. Then draw out threads to produce the lattice work effect. Usually two threads are drawn and three left. It is necessary to experiment to make sure the resulting holes are square. It is easiest to start counting and drawing threads half way along one side from both warp and weft. Hold the work over the index finger and draw up threads with the blunt pointed needle about 2 inches from the edge (see page 16). This will give you a better grip to draw out the rest of the thread and also enable you to check that the right threads have been drawn; if this is not the case, the short ends can easily be woven in again. After the threads are drawn from both warp and weft, the material will look like a chequerboard except at the edges, where it will look striped. It is this edge that is used for the hem. Now turn in the edges with a tacking thread so that the material will not fray. Press to make it smooth and even. As already mentioned, a piece of pin board is now used to stretch the material over instead of the traditional birch bark, and this must be

1 inch larger than the completed work.

To make sure that you can see the groups of thread easily, first cover the board with coloured paper, plastic, adhesive paper or closely woven fabric. Then stretch the work tightly over the pin board with pins, preferably glass headed ones (see page 17 where the pins are shown). The stitch with a strong thread and a strong pointed needle. It is easy to stitch into the soft cardboard-like substance. By stitching the fabric to the back of the board, it will lie firmly in place and there will be no edges to get in the way while working.

Beginners who need to see the right side of the work may use a sheet of perspex instead of the pinboard but this must have holes drilled along the edge at $\frac{1}{2}$ inch intervals.

Threads being drawn out of the fabric.

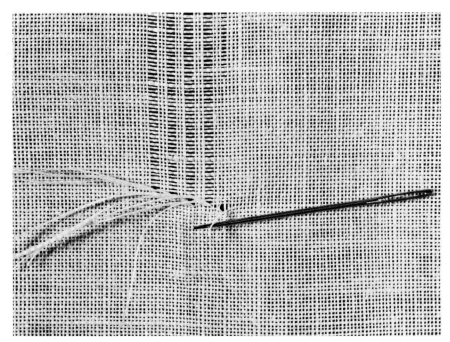

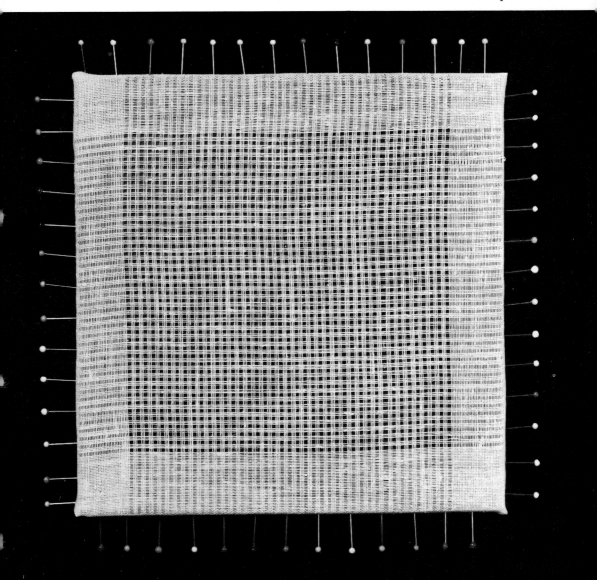

The material stretched out on the pin board.

TECHNIQUE

Drawn threadwork is worked in four different stitches, each of which forms a ground. Darning stitch and diagonal stitch are both known as 'closed groundwork', while goose-eye and ground stitch are known as 'open groundwork'. It is best to do all the darning stitch first and then go on to the diagonal stitch. Goose-eye and ground stitch tend to pull the work, so it is better to work these last. As the work is always done with the wrong side uppermost, it is important to fasten ends of threads carefully and make sure that no fastening stitches are visible from the right side.

Darning stitch

To begin working the darning and diagonal stitches, attach the thread as shown on page 19. The thread is normally used double and is attached by threading the needle through the end loop. A border in darning stitch is started at a corner and is worked from right to left. If a thread has to be joined, try to follow the outlines of a pattern shape. The join must be as invisible as possible. When working borders, it is best to try and start with a new thread in a corner as it will be less conspicuous.

The finer single thread used in ground stitch and goose-eye may be fastened into the edge of the darning stitch or diagonal stitch, or into an edging border. Joins may be made by means of a lace knot, or by twisting the two ends together, later fastening in the ends as invisibly as possible.

Corners may be worked in various ways, and a number of suggestions are shown on pages 20–23.

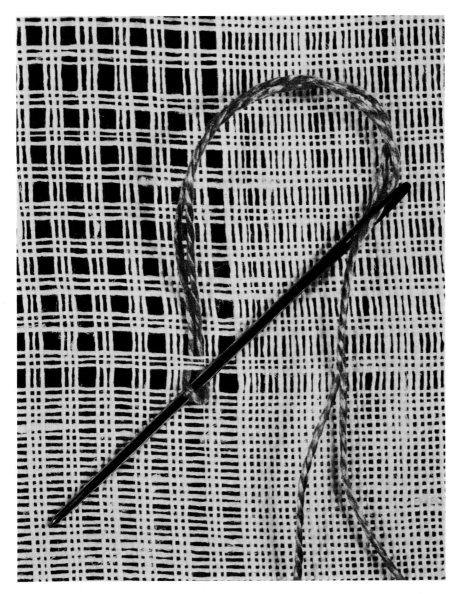

Starting the darning stitch.

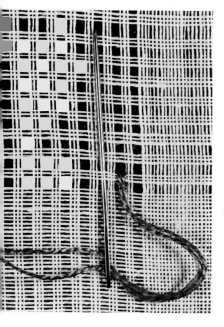

Left. The first hole is always missed so that the pattern will fit symmetrically into the corner.

Right. A border worked as an edging may be over two or more groups of threads. This shows how the thread is darned over and under the groups of threads according to the pattern required.

Below. A border, on the wrong side, worked in darning stitch where the threads have been joined at the corner by dividing them and working each one into the edges.
Below. The same border on the right side.

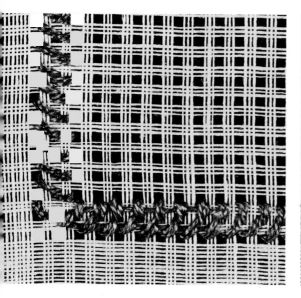

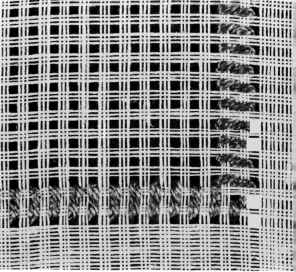

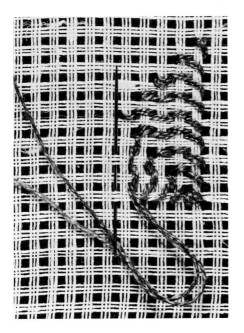

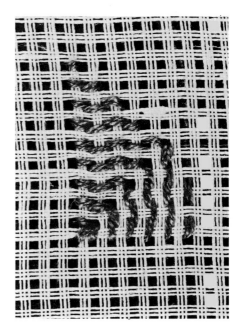

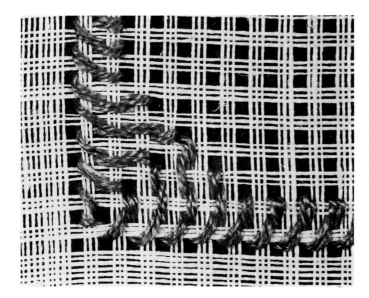

Above. The thread has been worked into the corner space.
Left. The wrong side.
Right. The right side.

Left. An example of a corner with the darning stitch worked over a number of groups of threads.

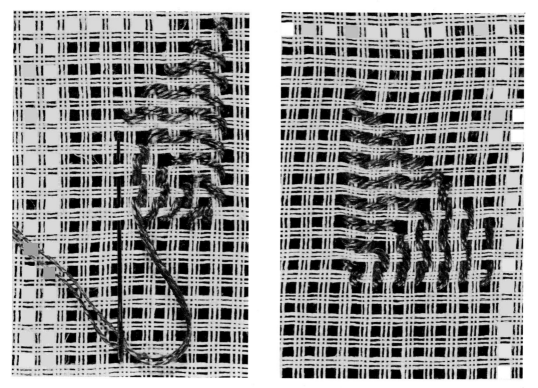

The corner hole has been left free.
Left. The wrong side.   Right. The right side.

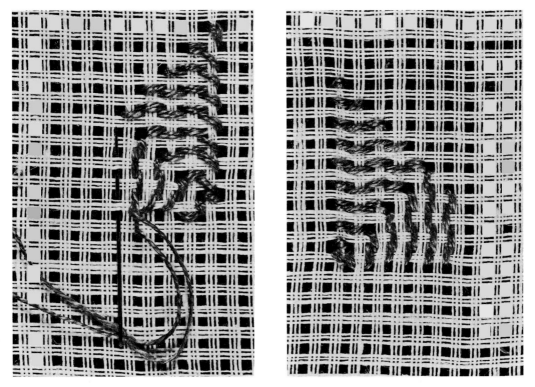

The thread has been carried across the corner threads.
Left. The wrong side.   Right. The right side.

The pattern darning may be increased as shown in the illustrations above and below which show two different methods.

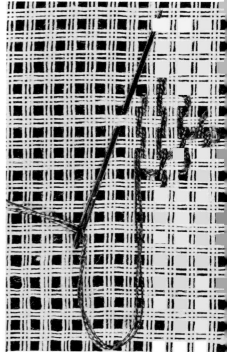

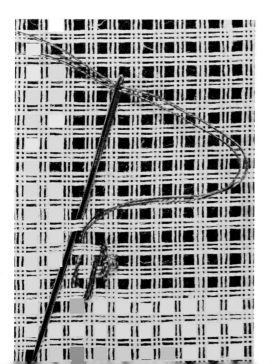

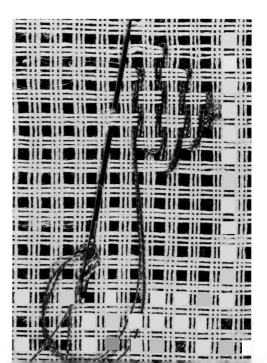

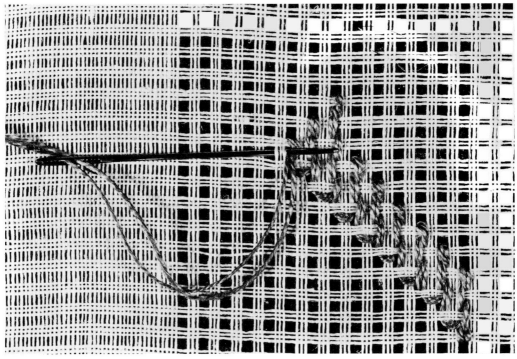

When working a diamond in darning stitch it is best to begin at
the lower corner, work as shown in the illustrations and take
three darning stitches into the holes in the top corner.

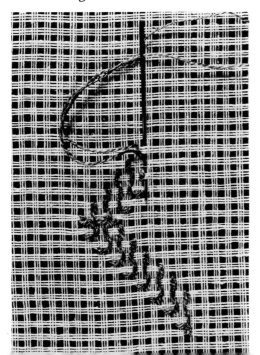 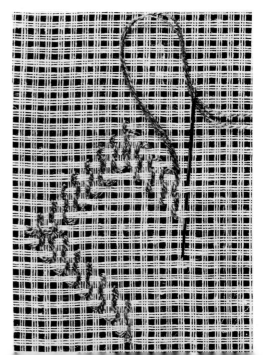

Diagonal stitch

Diagonal stitch is made by darning over two groups of threads, working diagonally from right to left and from the lower threads upwards. As with the darning stitch, diagonal stitch is worked with double thread and is attached to the fabric in the same way. The thread forms a continuous diagonal line, which gives diagonal stitch a completely different effect from darning stitch. As you can see from the illustrations when the pattern changes direction, the work is turned.

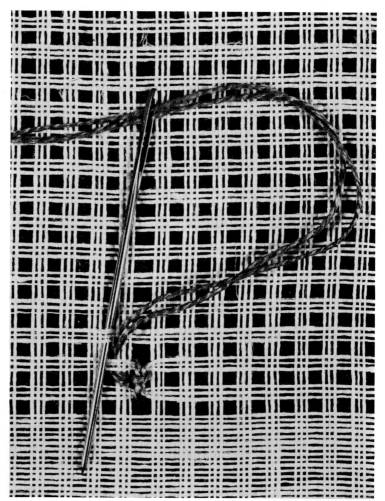

Above right. Diagonal stitch showing a change of direction.
Right. Diagonal stitch on the right side.

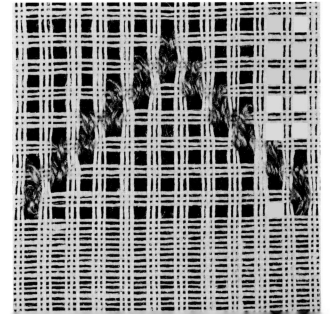

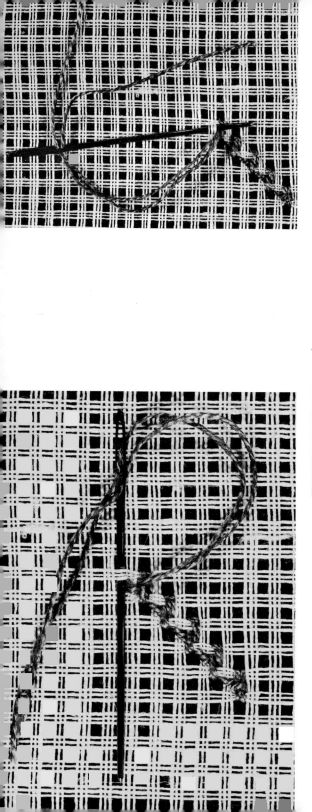

It is often necessary to change direction in diagonal stitch in the middle of a panel. These illustrations show how this is done.

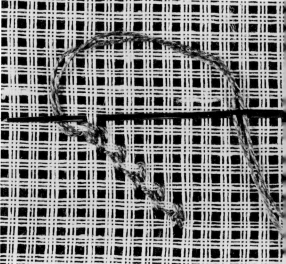

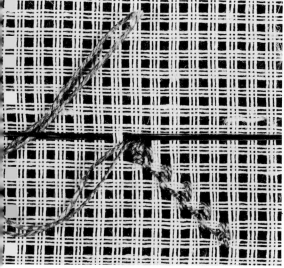

Note that the thread which forms a continuous diagonal line can lie on either the inside or the outside of the diagonal stitch. It is necessary to be consistent.

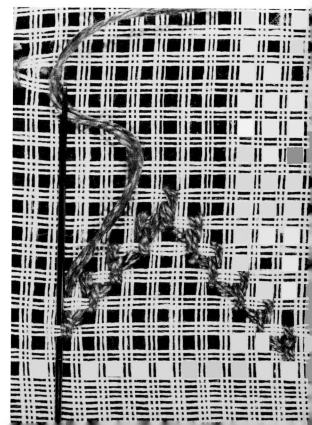

Goose-eye stitch

Goose-eye stitch is worked over two groups of threads alternately horizontally and vertically. It is always worked diagonally from left to right and from the lower threads upwards. The work is turned sideways by a quarter turn when the pattern changes direction. Each group of threads is always whipped twice to make the work firmer and the pattern more clearly defined.

Below right. The work is turned sideways by a quarter turn when the pattern changes direction.

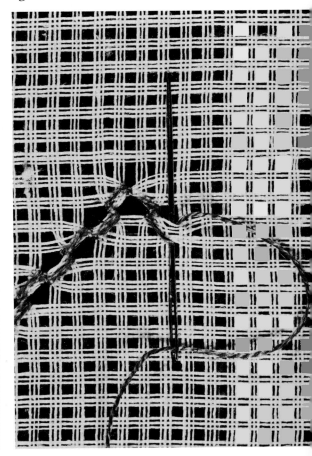

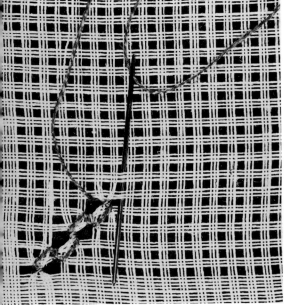

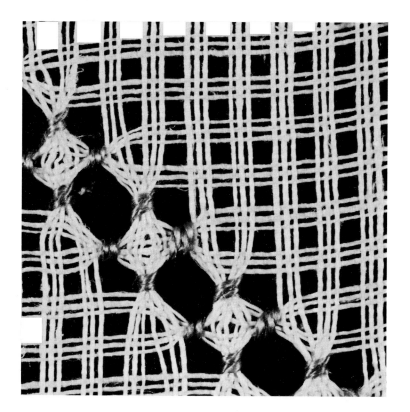

Above. The working of a second row of goose-eye stitch.

Right. Goose-eye stitch on the right side.

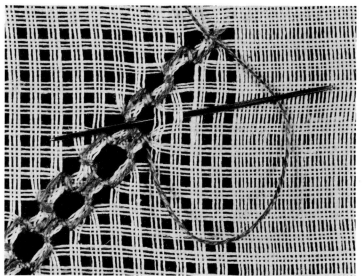

Ground stitch

Ground stitch is worked with a single thread. To start it is best to leave an end of about 2 inches long which is fastened into the hem later. Ground stitch is worked with straight stitches on the wrong side, which gives diagonal stitches on the right side. It is worked from right to left, diagonally from the top downwards, and turned by a half turn clockwise when you have reached the end of a row, at the lower edge of the area to be worked in this stitch.

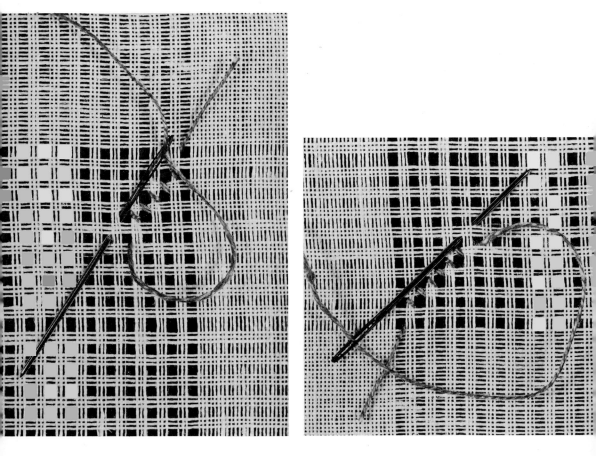

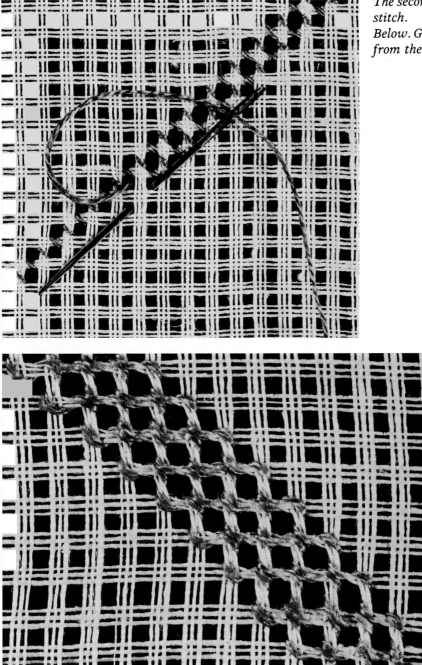

The second row of ground stitch.
Below. Ground stitch seen from the right side.

33

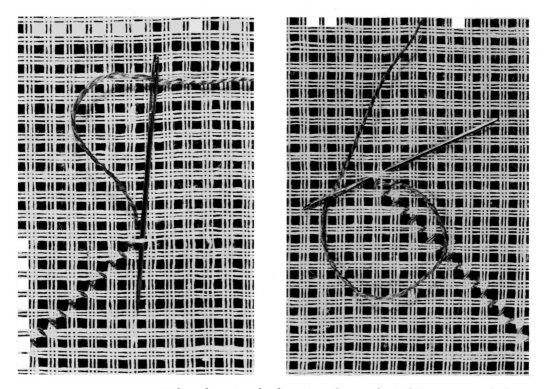

When changing the direction of ground stitch in a corner, the best way is to insert the needle under a single thread, one of the three in the group of threads, and then diagonally under the next intersection.

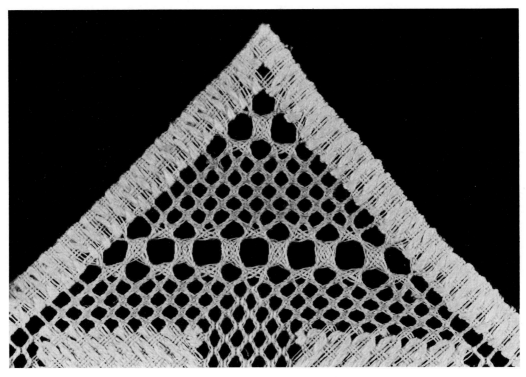

Detail of how the thread is carried round in ground stitch.

Samplers

To practise the different stitches properly it is advisable to make samplers, for which a suitable size of board is 12 inches square. This allows room for all four stitches. These small areas may be used later to make items such as mats, needlebooks or purses. The illustrations show samplers on which all four stitches have been worked.

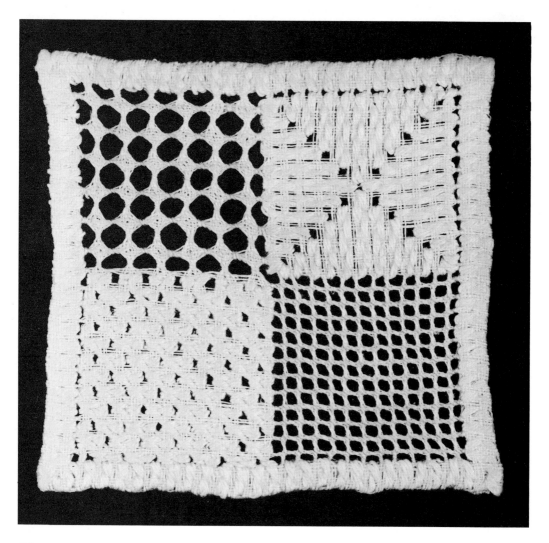

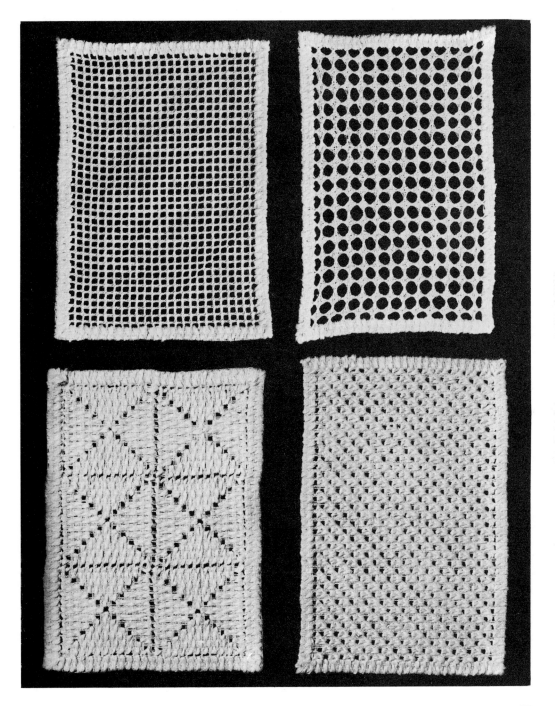

How to mitre a corner.

MAKING UP

When the work is finished, provided that the board is covered with a material of fast colour, a damp towel is placed on it, preferably with a weight on the top. After a few hours, when the work is dry, it can be removed from the board. If the threads at the edges are misplaced and uneven, as may easily happen because in drawn thread-work the threads are pulled together, one or two threads at the edges may be carefully straightened. The finishing off is a very important part of the final effect. Hems and corners must be neatened with great care. Right-angled corners are the most suitable for drawn threadwork. Hems should be turned in twice to prevent any raw edges showing, and the hems will also be firmer this way. If a narrow border has been worked in darning stitch over two groups of threads, it is best to use single hemstitching. If the border is wider, neaten the hem with ordinary hemming with the stitches into the second row of darning stitch. For hemming use a fine sewing thread and a fine sharp pointed needle.

Cushions, bags, purses, spectacle cases and lampshades must be very carefully made up. Inaccurate work can spoil the whole effect. When making up cushions, make a cover of fine linen, either matching the drawn threadwork or in a contrasting colour, and stitch the cushion padding into this. Then cut out a piece of linen of the same quality and size as the embroidery and stitch the two together round three sides from the wrong side. Turn inside out, press out the corners with the fingers, put the padding inside and stitch up the fourth side invisibly. To give a neat finish, stitch a cord all round the edge. This should be made of several strands of the same thread that was used for the drawn threadwork.

To mount bags and purses on to frames, the lining must be cut the same size as the outer cover and the two stitched up separately with small stitches. The bag is then stitched to the lining at the top and attached to the inside of the frame. It is difficult to make these mounting stitches invisible and it is best to cover them with a cord made of several strands of thread.

Spectacle cases require a framework of cardboard or tailor's canvas, two pieces of which should be cut out in the shape required. Four pieces of fine lining material are then cut out either matching or contrasting to the drawn threadwork. Turnings must be allowed on each piece of lining which should be stitched securely over the stiffening. The embroidery is then stitched on to one of the pieces and the two oversewn firmly together. Here again the appearance will be improved if the join is covered with a tightly twisted cord.

Envelope bags should be made up with a stiffening of a double thickness of tailor's canvas, foam rubber or heavy Vilene. The simplest way is to make up the lining material together with the stiffening as a separate bag, and insert this into the completed outer bag.

Washing advice

Drawn threadwork must be washed with the greatest care. Measure it accurately before washing so that the size may be kept the same. Use soap flakes and rinse thoroughly. Lay the work between two towels to remove most of the moisture. Then stretch it out, right side downwards on some soft surface, for example, an ironing board or pin board covered with a white cloth, and pin closely along the edges, using rust-proof pins. Then lay a dry towel over it, preferably with a weight on top. In a few hours, when the work feels dry, remove the pins and it will be smooth.

Further details can be found in *Mounting Handicraft* by Grete Kroncke published by Van Nostrand Reinhold.

ORIGINAL DESIGNS

In making your own pattern it is important to use shapes that are suitable for the drawn threadwork technique. The geometrical shapes which are easiest to work with are the square, the rectangle and the triangle. Using a sheet of white paper, draw the outline of the design to the required size. Cut out shapes in coloured paper and experiment by arranging these on the white paper until you decide upon a design. When transferring the design to lined paper use graph paper with 10 squares to the inch and either use it as it is or rule pencil lines in the centre of alternative squares in both directions to represent the holes and threads of the prepared fabric. In the latter each group of threads is clearly marked and it is easy to sketch in the design.

To obtain the correct size for the proposed work, multiply the size of the design by the number of holes per inch of the prepared linen. This simple calculation will give the number of spaces required.

Example   Mat 8 inches × 8 inches
Material   34 threads per inch has 7 spaces to the inch
Result   8 × 7 = 56 spaces

Sketch in the darning stitch and diagonal stitch first and then fill in the spaces with goose-eye and ground stitch. Remember that in goose-eye the groups of threads are counted in even pairs and that a complete 'goose-eye' uses four sets of threads. If it is difficult to fit in the goose-eyes add or deduct one row of ground stitch.

A pattern showing cut paper shapes in position.

The same pattern transferred on to the specially prepared graph paper.

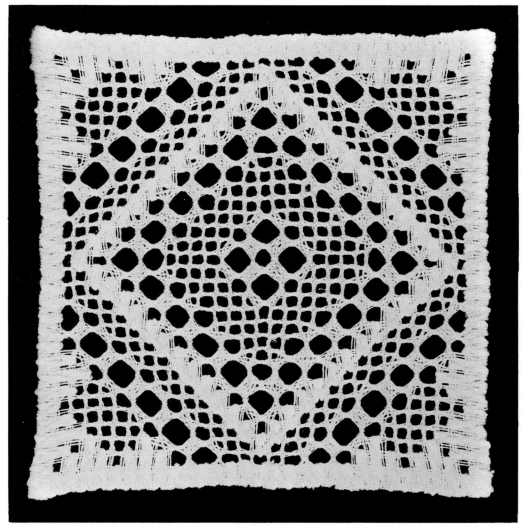

The finished embroidery.

DARNING STITCH

DIAGONAL STITCH

GOOSE-EYE STITCH

GROUND STITCH

Key to stitches sketched on to ordinary graph paper.

DARNING STITCH

DIAGONAL STITCH

GOOSE-EYE STITCH

GROUND STITCH

Key to stitches sketched on to specially prepared graph paper.

A design of cut paper.

Opposite top. The same design transferred on to ordinary graph paper.

Opposite bottom. The finished embroidery.

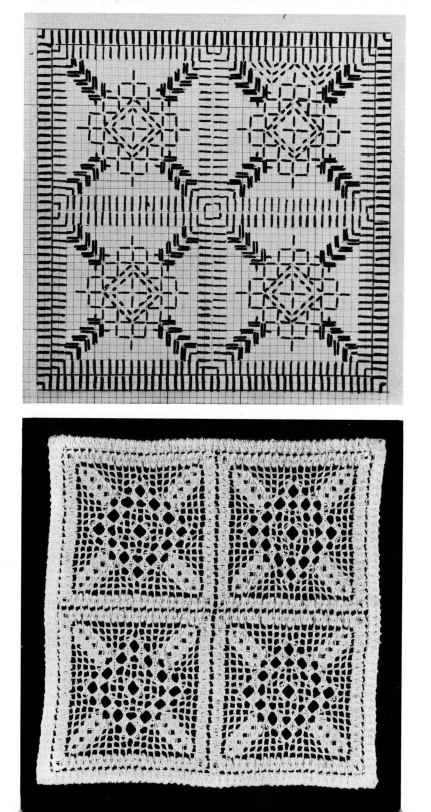

DESIGNS Mat

Size of material. 10 inches $\times$ 10 inches.
Spaces. 49 $\times$ 49
Evenweave linen 34 threads to the inch.
Heavy thread for darning stitch and diagonal stitch.
Fine thread for ground stitch and goose-eye stitch.

Mat

Size of material. 10 inches × 10 inches.
Spaces. 51 × 51
Evenweave linen 34 threads to the inch.
Heavy thread for darning stitch and diagonal stitch.
Fine thread for ground stitch and goose-eye stitch.

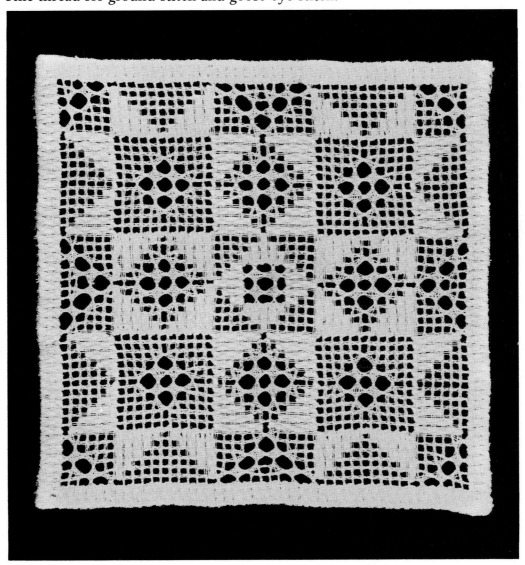

Mat

Size of material. $13\frac{3}{4}$ inches $\times$ $13\frac{3}{4}$ inches.

Spaces. 77 $\times$ 77

Evenweave linen 34 threads to the inch.

Heavy thread for darning stitch and diagonal stitch.

Fine thread for ground stitch and goose-eye stitch.

Mat

Size of material. $13\frac{3}{4}$ inches $\times$ $13\frac{3}{4}$ inches.

Spaces. 77 $\times$ 77

Evenweave linen 34 threads to the inch.

Heavy thread for darning stitch and diagonal stitch.

Fine thread for ground stitch and goose-eye stitch.

Mat

Size of material. $13\frac{3}{4}$ inches $\times$ $13\frac{3}{4}$ inches.

Spaces. 65 $\times$ 65

Evenweave linen 34 threads to the inch.

Heavy thread for darning stitch and diagonal stitch.

Fine thread for ground stitch and goose-eye stitch.

Mat

Size of material. $13\frac{3}{4}$ inches $\times$ $13\frac{3}{4}$ inches.

Spaces. 77×77

Evenweave linen 34 threads to the inch.

Heavy thread for darning stitch and diagonal stitch.

Fine thread for ground stitch and goose-eye stitch.

Mat
Size of material. 13¾ inches × 13¾ inches.
Spaces. 77 × 77
Evenweave linen 34 threads to the inch.
Heavy thread for darning stitch and diagonal stitch.
Fine thread for ground stitch and goose-eye stitch.

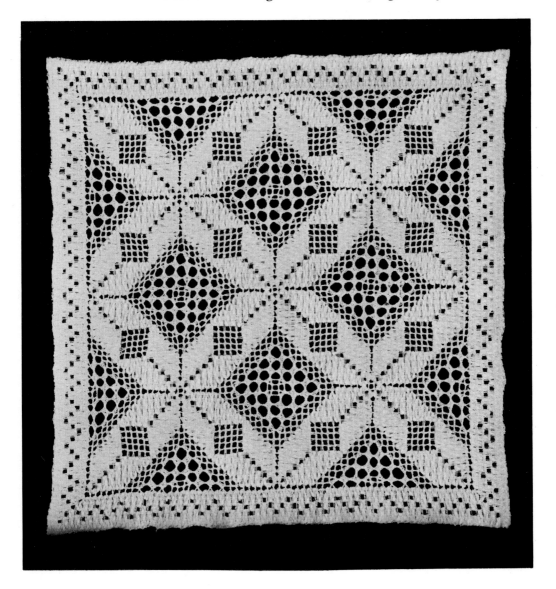

Mat

Size of material. 13¾ inches × 13¾ inches.
Spaces. 73 × 73
Evenweave linen 34 threads to the inch.
Heavy thread for darning stitch and diagonal stitch.
Fine thread for ground stitch and goose-eye stitch.

Mat
Size of material. 12 inches × 12 inches.
Spaces. 63 × 63
Evenweave linen 34 threads to the inch.
Heavy thread for darning stitch and diagonal stitch.
Fine thread for ground stitch and goose-eye stitch.

Mat

Size of material. 12 inches × 12 inches.
Spaces. 67 × 67
Evenweave linen 34 threads to the inch.
Heavy thread for darning stitch and diagonal stitch.
Fine thread for ground stitch and goose-eye stitch.

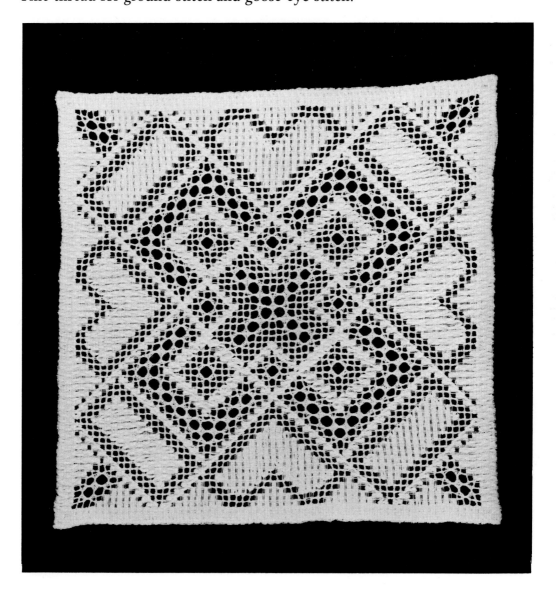

Table runner

Size of material. $13\frac{3}{4}$ inches $\times$ $25\frac{1}{2}$ inches.

Spaces. 71×151

Evenweave linen 34 threads to the inch.

Heavy thread for darning stitch and diagonal stitch.

Fine thread for ground stitch and goose-eye stitch.

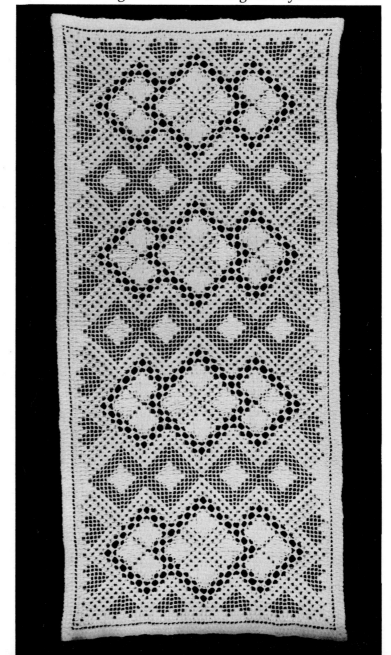

Mat

Size of material. $15\frac{3}{4}$ inches $\times$ $15\frac{3}{4}$ inches.

Spaces. 89×89

Evenweave linen 34 threads to the inch.

Heavy thread for darning stitch and diagonal stitch.

Fine thread for ground stitch and goose-eye stitch.

Mat

Size of material. $15\frac{3}{4}$ inches $\times$ $15\frac{3}{4}$ inches.

Spaces. 89×89

Evenweave linen 34 threads to the inch.

Heavy thread for darning stitch and diagonal stitch.

Fine thread for ground stitch and goose-eye stitch.

Mat

Size of material. 10 inches × 10 inches.
Spaces. 49 × 49
Evenweave linen 34 threads to the inch.
Heavy thread for darning stitch and diagonal stitch.
Fine thread for ground stitch and goose-eye stitch.

Cushion

Size of material. 13¾ inches × 13¾ inches.

Spaces. 81 × 81

Evenweave linen 34 threads to the inch.

Heavy thread for darning stitch and diagonal stitch.

Fine thread for ground stitch and goose-eye stitch.

Opposite. Detail of the work.

63

Cushion *(Opposite)*
Size of material. $13\frac{3}{4}$ inches $\times$ $13\frac{3}{4}$ inches.
Spaces. 77×77
Evenweave linen 34 threads to the inch.
Heavy thread for darning stitch and diagonal stitch.
Fine thread for ground stitch and goose-eye stitch.

Display panel *(Below)*
Size of material. $17\frac{3}{4}$ inches $\times$ $17\frac{3}{4}$ inches.
Spaces. 89×89
Evenweave linen 30 threads to the inch.
Heavy thread for darning stitch and diagonal stitch.
Fine thread for ground stitch and goose-eye stitch.

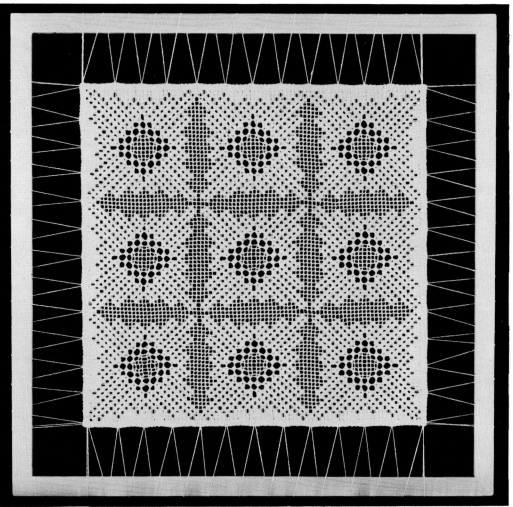

Mat
Size of material. 17¾ inches × 17¾ inches.
Spaces. 93 × 93
Evenweave linen 30 threads to the inch.
Heavy thread for darning stitch and diagonal stitch.
Fine thread for ground stitch and goose-eye stitch.

Mat

Size of material. $13\frac{3}{4}$ inches $\times$ $13\frac{3}{4}$ inches.

Spaces. 83×83

Evenweave linen 34 threads to the inch.

Heavy thread for darning stitch and diagonal stitch.

Fine thread for ground stitch and goose-eye stitch.

Purse

Size of material. 8 inches $\times$ 12 inches.

Spaces. 41 $\times$ 65

Evenweave linen 34 threads to the inch.

Heavy thread for darning stitch and diagonal stitch.

Fine thread for ground stitch and goose-eye stitch.

Opposite. Detail of the work.

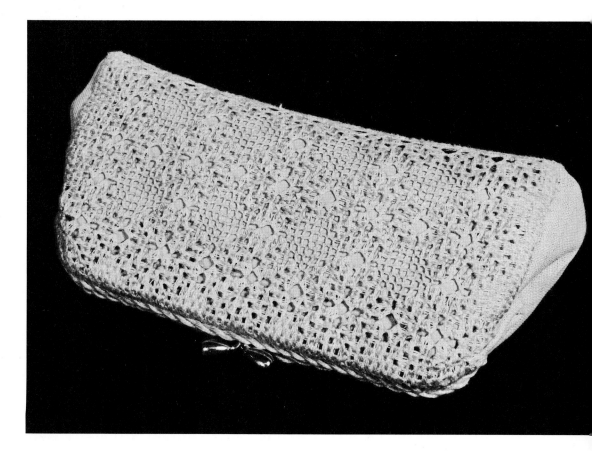

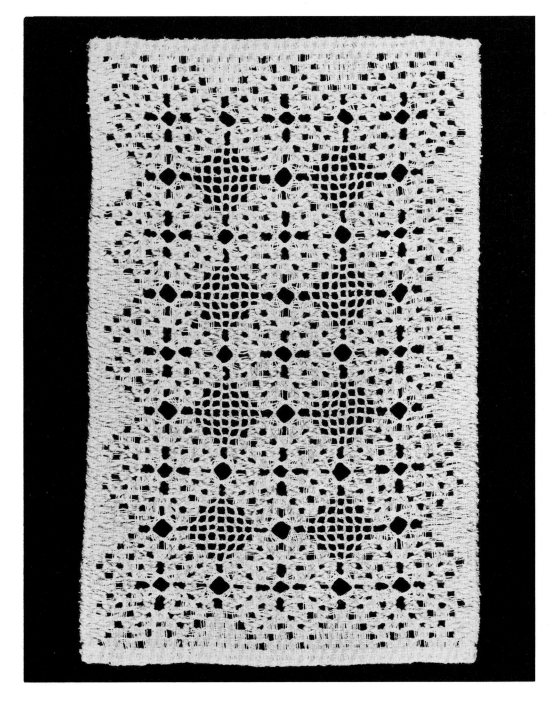

Purse

Size of material. 6 inches × 6 inches.
Spaces. 28 × 31
Evenweave linen 34 threads to the inch.
Heavy thread for darning stitch and diagonal stitch.
Fine thread for ground stitch and goose-eye stitch.

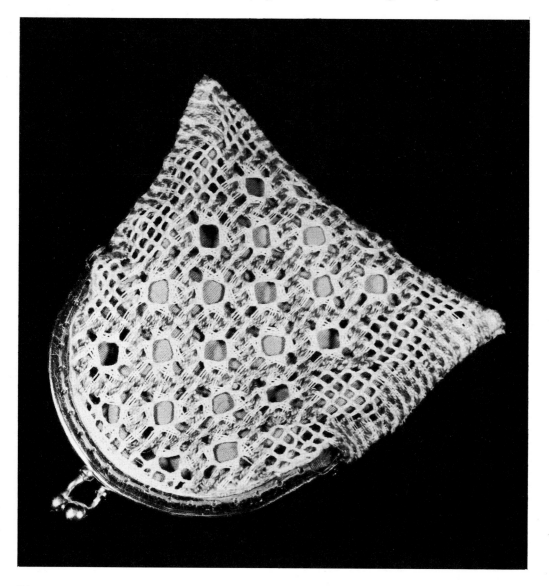

Purse

Size of material. 8 inches $\times$ 8 inches.
Spaces. 33 $\times$ 33
Evenweave linen 34 threads to the inch.
Heavy thread for darning stitch and diagonal stitch.
Fine thread for ground stitch and goose-eye stitch.

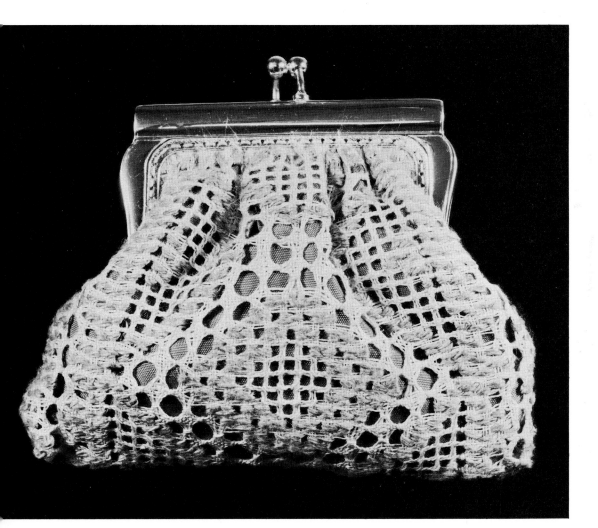

Shopping bag
Size of material. $17\frac{3}{4}$ inches $\times$ $17\frac{3}{4}$ inches.
Spaces. 71×71
Evenweave linen 34 threads to the inch.
Heavy thread for darning stitch and diagonal stitch.
Fine thread for ground stitch and goose-eye stitch.
Opposite. Detail of the work.

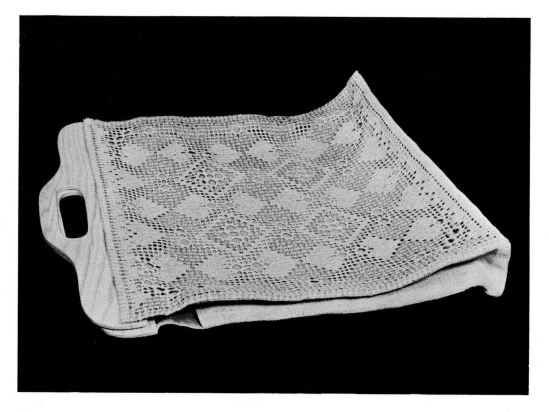

Handbag

Size of material. 10 inches $\times$ 13$\frac{3}{4}$ inches.
Spaces. 53 $\times$ 61
Evenweave linen 34 threads to the inch.
Heavy thread for darning stitch and diagonal stitch.
Fine thread for ground stitch and goose-eye stitch.

Evening bag
Size of material. 13¾ inches × 13¾ inches.
Spaces. 41 × 65
Evenweave linen 34 threads to the inch.
Heavy thread for darning stitch and diagonal stitch.
Fine thread for ground stitch and goose-eye stitch.

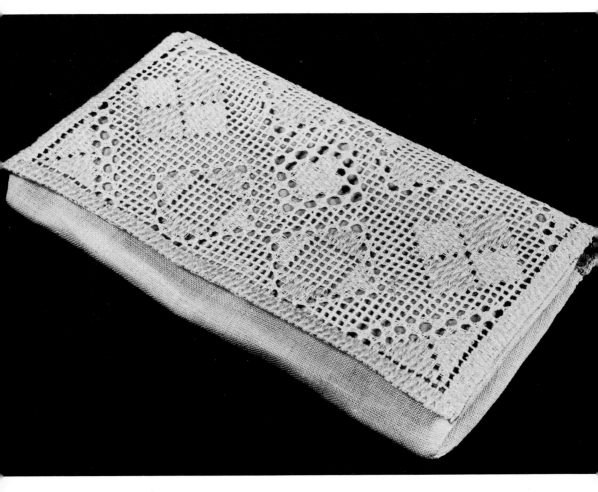

Evening bag *(Below)*
Size of material. 10 inches × 10
inches.
Spaces. 53 × 61
Evenweave linen 34 threads to the
inch.
Heavy thread for darning stitch
and diagonal stitch.
Fine thread for ground stitch and
goose-eye stitch.

Spectacle case *(Opposite)*
Size of material. 4 inches × 8
inches.
Spaces. 21 × 53
Evenweave linen 34 threads to the
inch.
Heavy thread for darning stitch
and diagonal stitch.
Fine thread for ground stitch.

Spectacle case
Size of material. 10 inches × 10 inches.
Spaces. 44 × 49
Evenweave linen 34 threads to the inch.
Heavy thread for darning stitch and diagonal stitch.
Fine thread for ground stitch.

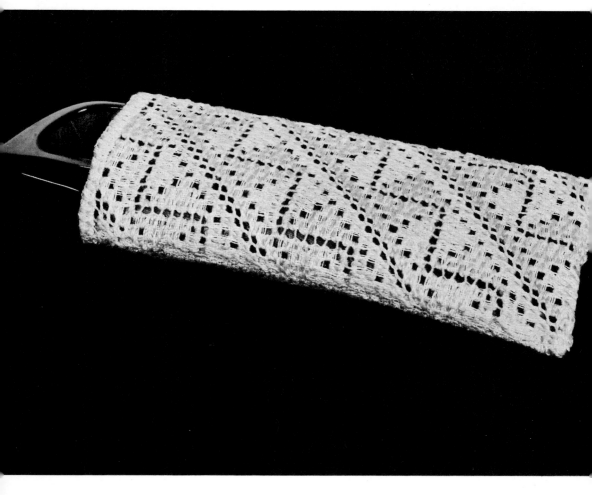

Mat
Size of material. 15¾ inches × 15¾ inches.
Spaces. 98 × 98
Evenweave linen 23 threads to the inch.
Heavy thread for darning stitch.
Fine thread for ground stitch and goose-eye stitch.

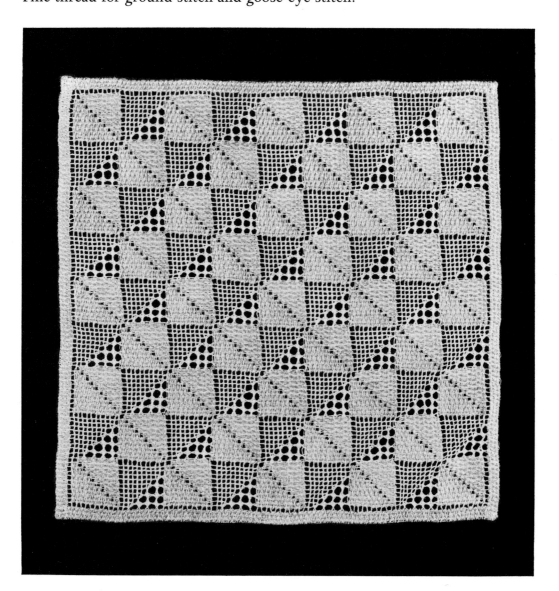

Lampshade

Size of material. 10 inches $\times$ $17\frac{3}{4}$ inches.

Spaces. 41 $\times$ 97

Evenweave linen 34 threads to the inch.

Heavy thread for darning stitch and diagonal stitch.

Fine thread for ground stitch and goose-eye stitch.

Opposite. Detail of the work.

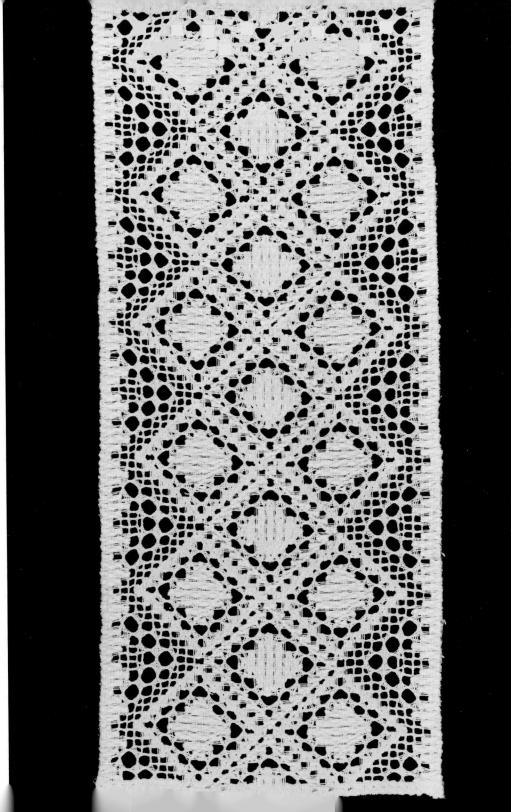

Lampshade

Size of material. $13\frac{3}{4}$ inches $\times$ $25\frac{1}{2}$ inches.
Spaces. 71×167
Evenweave linen 34 threads to the inch.
Heavy thread for darning stitch and diagonal stitch.
Fine thread for ground stitch and goose-eye stitch.
Opposite. Detail of the work.

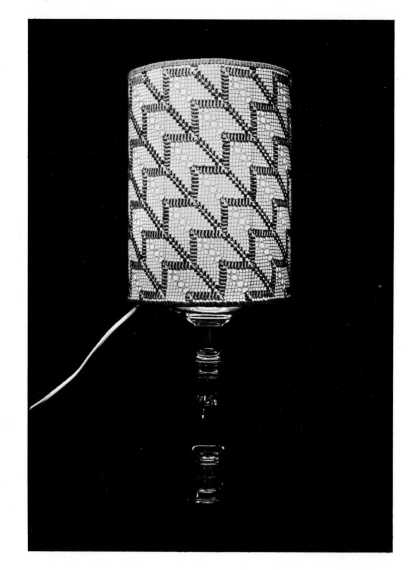

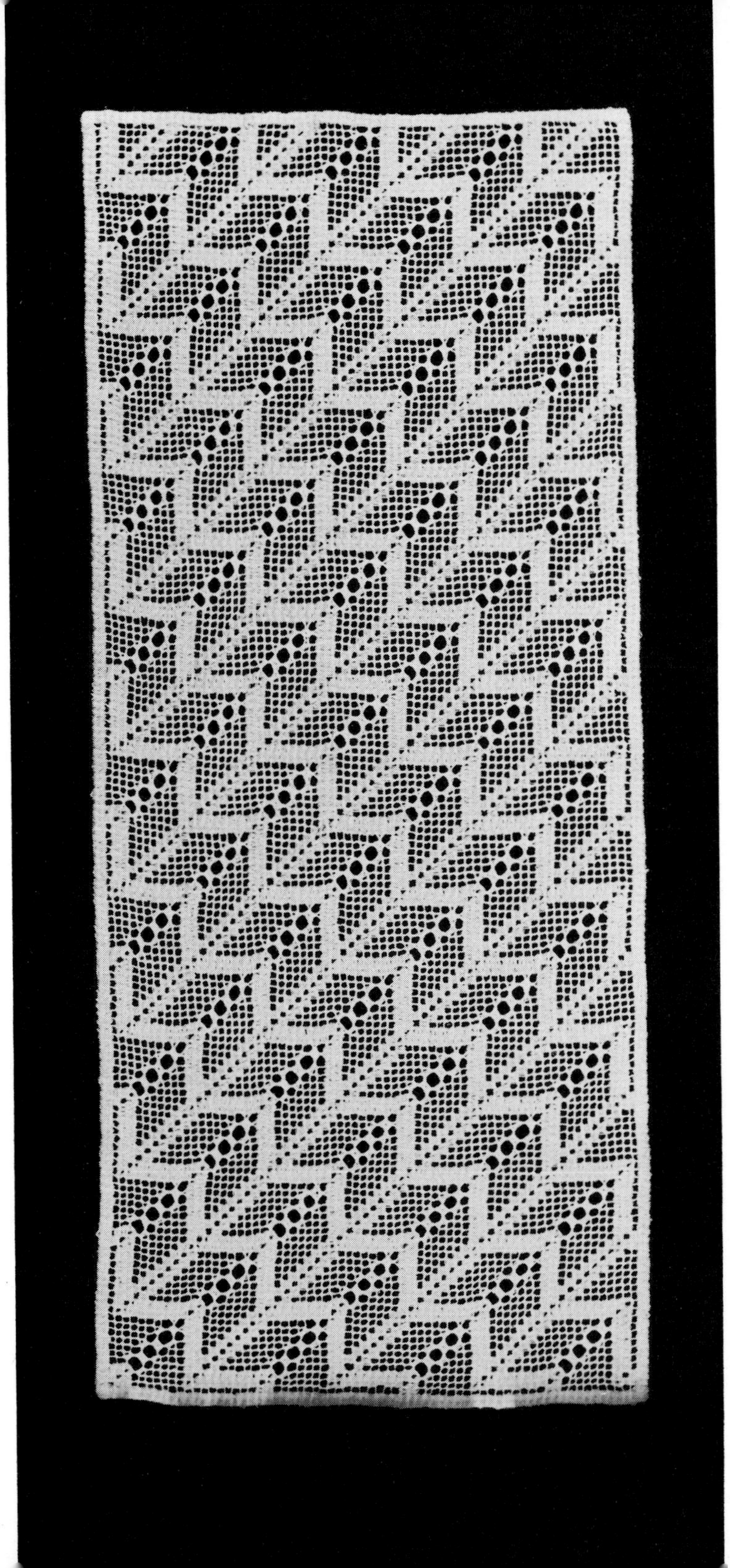

Lampshade

Size of material. 10 inches $\times$ 17$\frac{3}{4}$ inches.
Spaces. 45 $\times$ 101
Evenweave linen 34 threads to the inch.
Heavy thread for darning stitch and diagonal stitch.
Fine thread for ground stitch and goose-eye stitch.
Opposite. Detail of the work.

Lampshade

Size of material. $13\frac{3}{4}$ inches $\times$ $25\frac{1}{2}$ inches.

Spaces. 69×147

Evenweave linen 34 threads to the inch.

Heavy thread for darning stitch and diagonal stitch.

Fine thread for ground stitch and goose-eye stitch.

Lampshade

Size of material. 10 inches $\times$ 15$\frac{3}{4}$ inches.

Spaces. 41 $\times$ 95

Evenweave linen 34 threads to the inch.

Heavy thread for darning stitch and diagonal stitch.

Fine thread for ground stitch and goose-eye stitch.

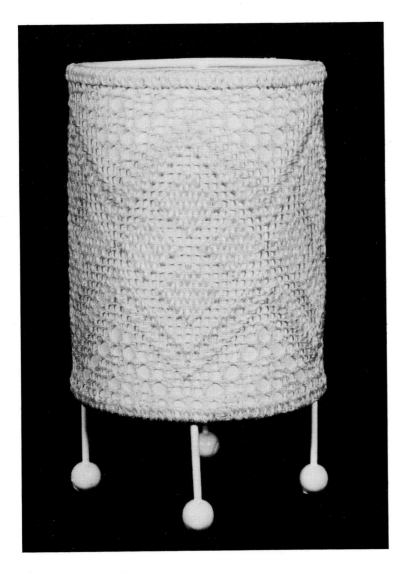

Glass mats
Size of material. 4 inches × 4 inches.
Spaces. 21 × 21
Evenweave linen 34 threads to the inch.
Heavy thread for darning stitch and diagonal stitch.
Fine thread for ground stitch and goose-eye stitch.

Display panel

Size of material. $17\frac{3}{4}$ inches $\times$ $17\frac{3}{4}$ inches.

Spaces. 87×87

Evenweave linen 30 threads to the inch.

Heavy thread for darning stitch and diagonal stitch

Fine thread for ground stitch and goose-eye stitch.

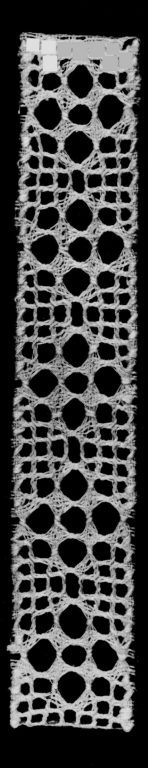
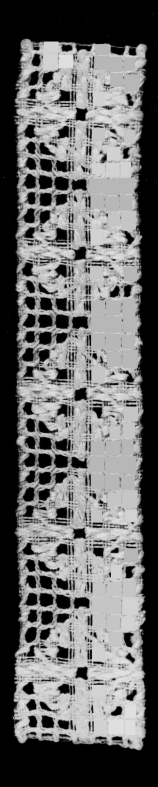

Book marks *(Opposite)*
Size of material. $1\frac{1}{4}$ inches $\times$ $5\frac{1}{2}$ inches.
Spaces. 9 $\times$ 41
Evenweave linen 34 threads to the inch.
Heavy thread for darning stitch and diagonal stitch.
Fine thread for ground stitch and goose-eye stitch.

Band *(Below)*
Size of material. 6 inches $\times$ $21\frac{3}{4}$ inches.
Spaces. 13 $\times$ 117
Evenweave linen 30 threads to the inch.
Heavy thread for darning stitch and diagonal stitch.
Fine thread for ground stitch and goose-eye stitch.

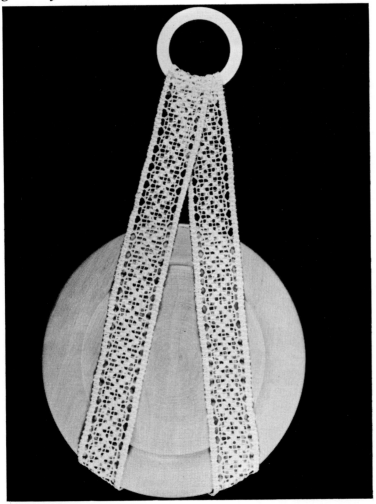

Handkerchief *(Below)*
Size of material. 13¾ inches × 13¾
inches.
Spaces. 21 × 81
Evenweave linen 34 threads to the
inch.
Heavy thread for darning stitch
and diagonal stitch.
Fine thread for ground stitch and
goose-eye stitch.

Table runner *(Opposite)*
Size of material. 8 inches × 29½
inches.
Spaces. 41 × 169
Evenweave linen 30 threads to the
inch.
Heavy thread for darning stitch
and diagonal stitch.
Fine thread for ground stitch and
goose-eye stitch.

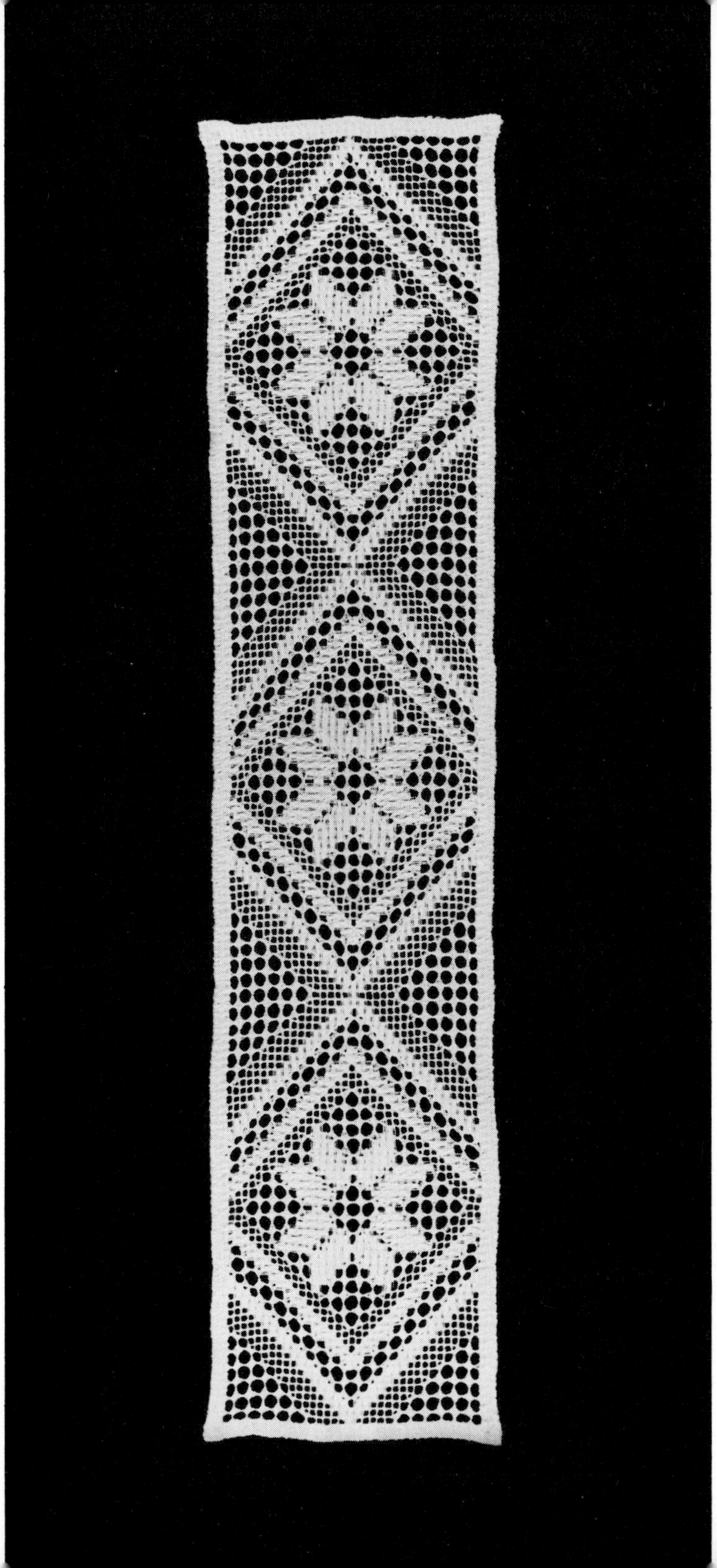

Decorated napkin *(Opposite)*
Size of material. 4 inches × 15¾
inches.
Spaces. 19 × 95
Evenweave linen 34 threads to the
inch.
Heavy thread for darning stitch
and diagonal stitch.
Fine thread for ground stitch and
goose-eye stitch.

Mat *(Below)*
Size of material. 10 inches × 10
inches
Spaces. 46 × 46
Evenweave linen 34 threads to the
inch.
Heavy thread for darning stitch.
Fine thread for goose-eye stitch.

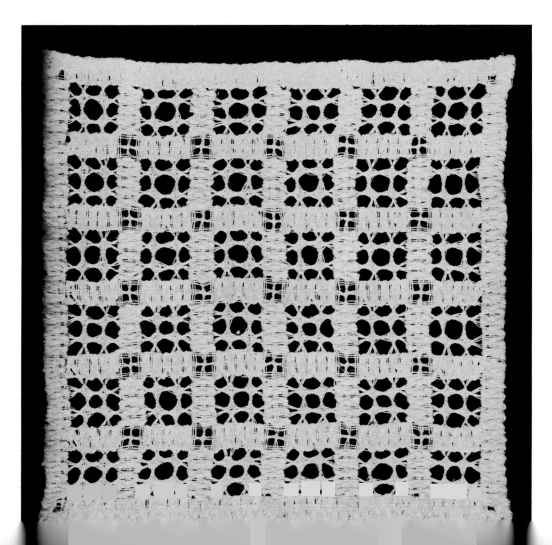

LIST OF SUPPLIERS

The Needlewoman Shop,
146 Regent Street,
London W.1,
England

Contessa Yarns,
P.O. Box 37,
Levanon,
Connecticut 06249,
U.S.A.

Frederick J. Fawcett, Inc.
129 South Street,
Boston,
Massachusetts 02111,
U.S.A.

Aktiebolaget Nordiska Kompaniet,
Box 7159,
Stockholm 7,
Sweden

Hemslojdforbundet for Sverige,
Sturegatan 29,
Stockholm,
Sweden

Skaraborgs Läns Hemslojdsforenings filial,
Gamla Rådhuset,
531 01 Lidköping,
Sweden